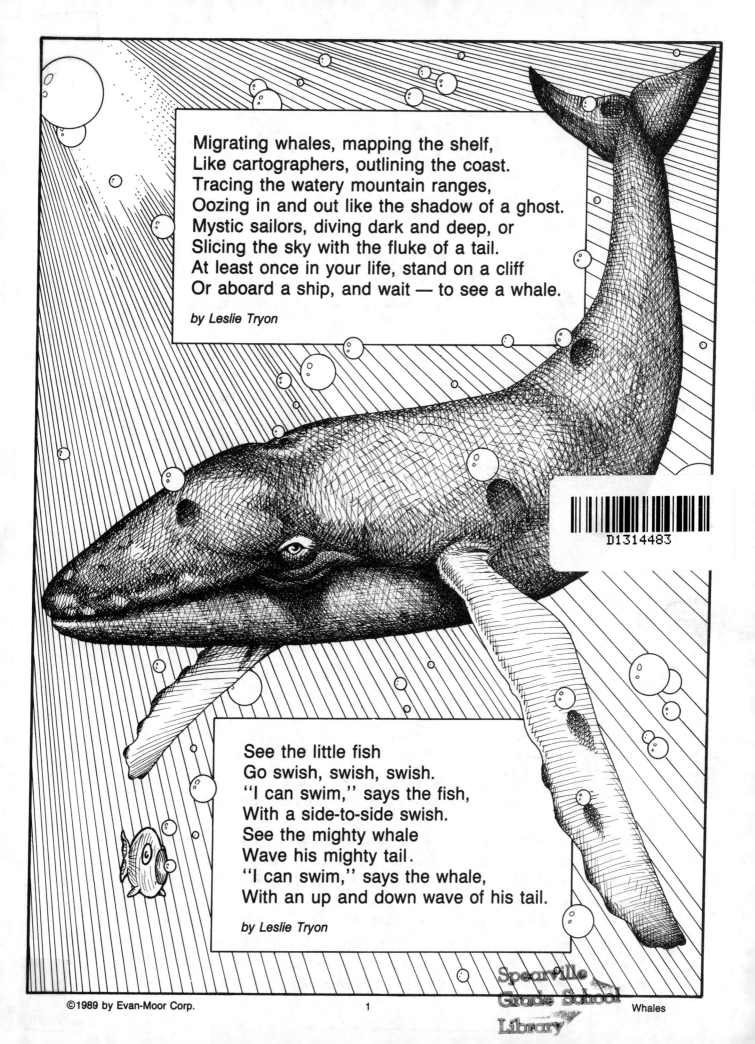

Migrating whales, mapping the shelf,
Like cartographers, outlining the coast.
Tracing the watery mountain ranges,
Oozing in and out like the shadow of a ghost.
Mystic sailors, diving dark and deep, or
Slicing the sky with the fluke of a tail.
At least once in your life, stand on a cliff
Or aboard a ship, and wait — to see a whale.

by Leslie Tryon

See the little fish
Go swish, swish, swish.
"I can swim," says the fish,
With a side-to-side swish.
See the mighty whale
Wave his mighty tail.
"I can swim," says the whale,
With an up and down wave of his tail.

by Leslie Tryon

Whales

Let's Learn About Whales

Read About Whales

All About Whales by Dorothy Henshaw Patent; Holiday House, 1987

An Educational Coloring Book of Whales, Linda Spizzirri, Editor; Spizzirri Publishing Co., 1982

A First Look at Whales by Millicent Selsam & Joyce Hunt; Walker & Co., 1980

A Pod of Gray Whales by Francois Gohier; Blake Publishing, 1988

A Year in the Life of a Whale by John Stidworthy; Silver Burdett, 1975

Great Whales by Patricia Lauber; Garrard, 1975

The Sea World Book of Whales by Eve Bunting; Harcourt Brace Jovanovich, 1980

Whales by John Bonnett Wexo; a Zoobook from Wildlife Education, Ltd., 1983

Whales: the Nomads of the Sea by Helen Roney Sattler; Lothrop, 1987

Whales of the World by June Behrens; Childrens Press, 1987

Note: This activity may be done as a whole group brain storming session or in cooperative-learning groups. Combine all information to create a large chart to leave up in class throughout the unit of study. Update the chart as the unit progresses.

Before We Begin

What we know about whales	What we want to learn about whales

Note: Use these illustrations to discuss the likenesses and differences between a whale and a fish. (This would be a good place to include the poem on page 1.)

A Whale is not a Fish

Although they share the same environment, there are important differences between a fish and a whale.

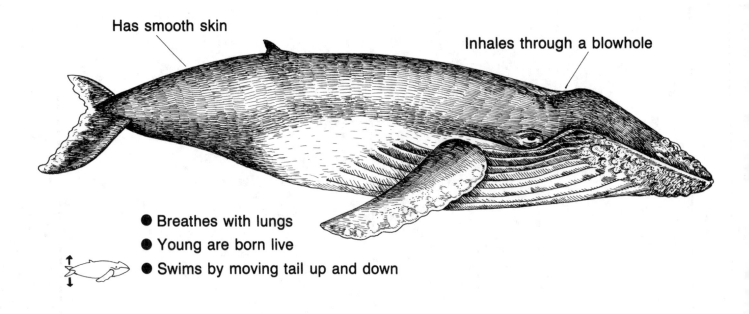

Has smooth skin

Inhales through a blowhole

● Breathes with lungs
● Young are born live
● Swims by moving tail up and down

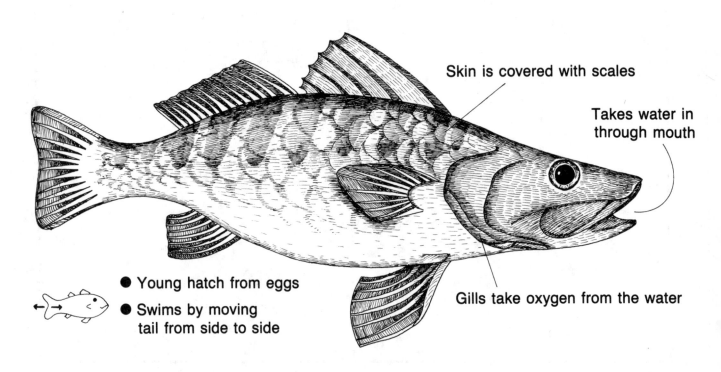

Skin is covered with scales

Takes water in through mouth

● Young hatch from eggs
● Swims by moving tail from side to side

Gills take oxygen from the water

Whales

Note: Children determine whether the statement is true of a whale, a fish, or both of the animals. You may want to do it as a ''thumbs up — thumbs down'' activity with younger children.

Whales or Fish?

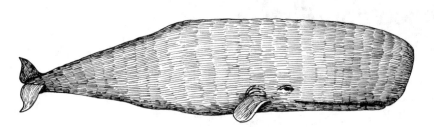 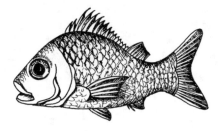

	whale	fish	both
1. skin is covered with scales			
2. lives in the sea			
3. young are born live			
4. has to come to the surface to breathe			
5. swims by moving its tail fin side to side			
6. is part of the animal kingdom			
7. some have baleen and some have teeth			
8. gills take oxygen from the water			
9. some sing as they swim through the water			
10. young hatch from eggs			
11. die if out of the water too long			
12. swims by moving tail fluke up and down			

Note: Begin Venn diagrams as a whole-group activity until children are comfortable making comparisons in this way.

Compare and Contrast
Whale and Fish

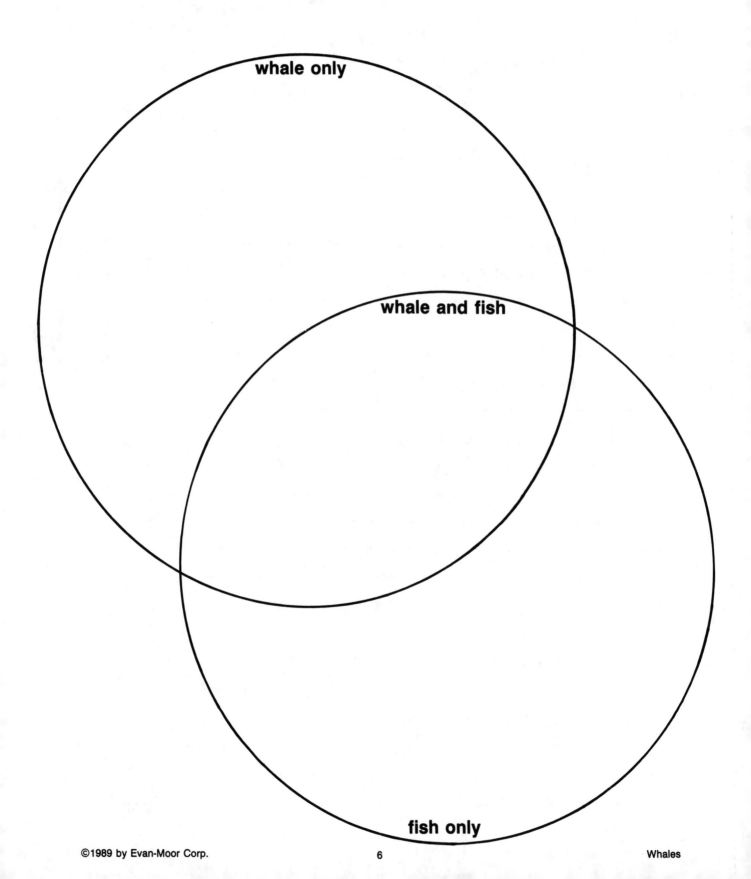

whale only

whale and fish

fish only

Whales

Whale Search

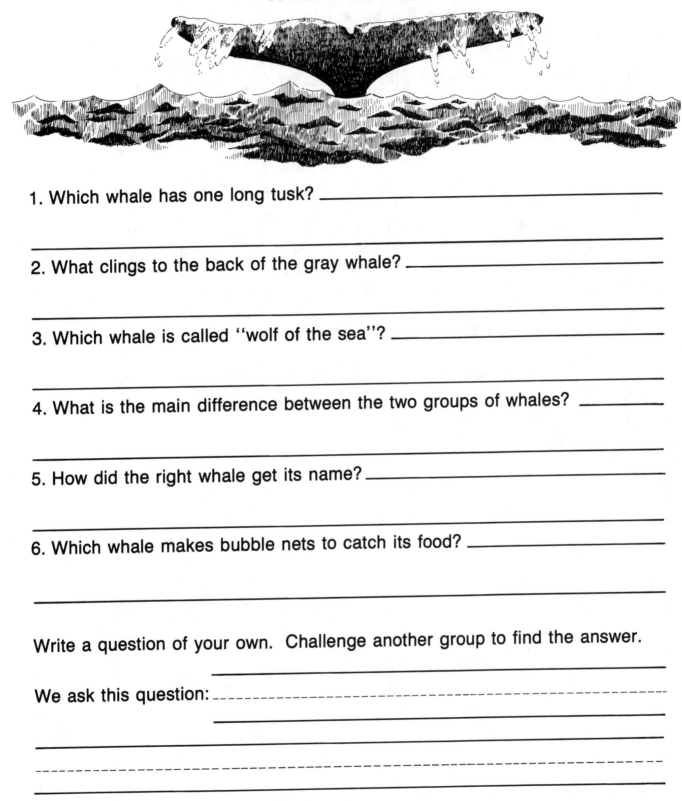

1. Which whale has one long tusk? _____

_____

2. What clings to the back of the gray whale? _____

_____

3. Which whale is called "wolf of the sea"? _____

_____

4. What is the main difference between the two groups of whales? ____

_____

5. How did the right whale get its name? _____

_____

6. Which whale makes bubble nets to catch its food? _____

_____

Write a question of your own. Challenge another group to find the answer.

We ask this question: _____

_____

_____

_____

The correct answer is: _____

_____

The other group (was — was not) able to find the answer to the question.

Life Cycle of the Whale

A whale baby is called a calf. Can you guess what the mother and father are called? That's right. The mother is a cow and the father is a bull. Whales usually have one baby at a time. The whale calf is born under water. It is born with its eyes open and ready to swim. The calf must go to the surface as soon as it is born in order to breathe. The mother helps the baby to the surface to take its first breath of air.

A whale calf grows very fast. Mother whale has nipples hidden in grooves on her belly. When the calf is hungry, it bumps its mother. She squirts milk into the baby's mouth. The baby whale can drink many gallons of milk in a short time. Whale milk is very rich. It looks more like cream than the milk you drink. Cow milk is 4 percent fat, while whale milk is more than 50 percent fat. Because its food is so rich, a whale calf grows very fast. A blue whale calf gains over eight pounds (four kilograms) each hour until it is several months old.

The whale calf will stay with its mother until it is able to find its own food.

Draw a mother whale and her calf.

Echolocation

It is hard to see very far under water. Light does not travel well through water, so the deeper you go, the darker it becomes.
Water is a good carrier of sound. In fact sound travels faster and farther in water than in air. Some whales have learned to "see" with sound. This is called echolocation.

The whale sends out a sound. When the sound hits an object such as rocks or a school of fish, it bounces back toward the whale.

The whale can tell how far off the object is by how long it takes the sound to bounce back.

Using echolocation helps these whales to find food and to avoid dangerous places.

Can you name another mammal that uses sound to find its way about?

Draw it here.

Migration

Many whales migrate from their cold homes to warmer areas to mate and give birth to their babies. For example, each year California gray whales migrate from the Arctic down to Mexican waters.

The gray whales spend the summer in the Arctic, swimming in the Bering and Chukchi Seas along the coast of Alaska and Siberia. When the weather begins to get chilly, they start down the Pacific coast. Late in December, the whales arrive off Baja California where they give birth to their babies. When spring arrives they head back north with their calves.

This is a long journey. It is more than 5,000 miles from the Arctic to the warm Mexican waters. The gray whale swims along at about 4-5 knots. This is about six miles per hour. It takes them about three months to travel each way.

Fill in the migration route of the California gray whale on the map on the following page.

Draw a mother and baby gray whale here.

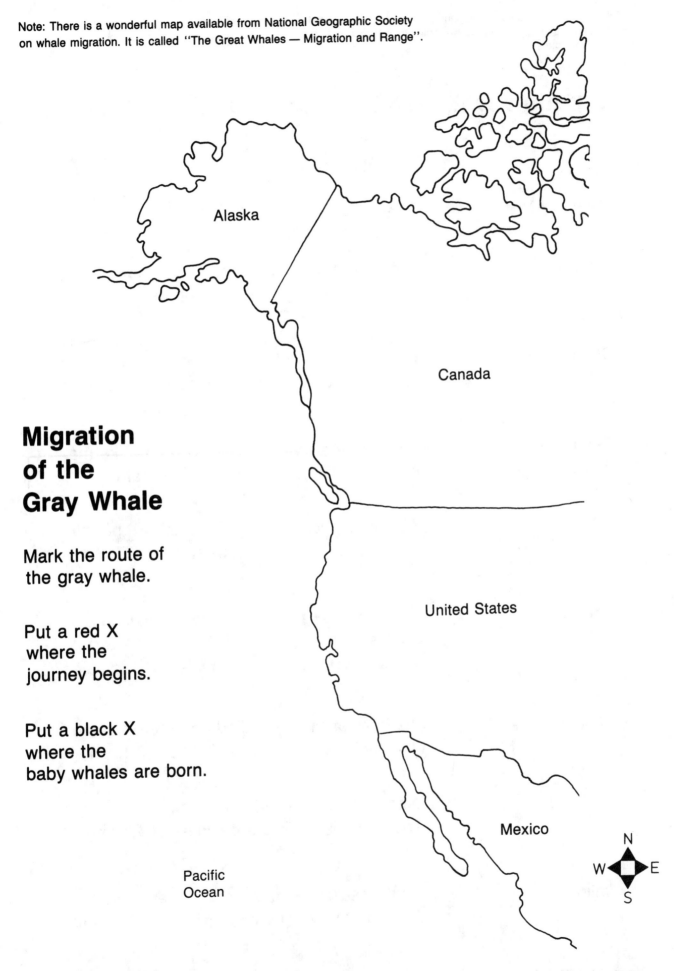

Note: There is a wonderful map available from National Geographic Society on whale migration. It is called "The Great Whales — Migration and Range".

Alaska

Canada

United States

Mexico

Migration of the Gray Whale

Mark the route of the gray whale.

Put a red X where the journey begins.

Put a black X where the baby whales are born.

Pacific Ocean

N
W E
S

Whales

Note: This skit on migration contains much information about whales. Any number of children can participate. It can be done by as few as two children asking and answering the questions or by the whole class by dividing into groups.

Migration of the Gray Whale — A Skit in Rhyme

by Leslie Tryon

Script

Character	Dialogue
Child 1	The sea is the avenue of transportation To whales ready to set out on migration.
Child 2	Why don't those fish stay put, like us? Why all that traveling? It's too much fuss.
Child 1	A whale is a mammal, like you and like me. And migration is a seasonal necessity. The bulls and the cows go south in the fall, As though they were answering a silent call.
Child 2	Bulls and cows? Weren't we discussing whales? Is that what they call the males and females?
Child 1	That's what they're called and there's more. I'll explain why whales swim along the shore. Whales as a rule migrate for breeding. They will also migrate because of feeding.
Child 2	Do they take the same route every time? Are they following some invisible road sign?

Continued on next page.

Script continued

Character	Dialogue
Child 1	Yes. They seem to know just where they're going. They all have an instinctive way of knowing.
	They go north in summer to the Arctic Sea. In winter the tropics is where they'll be.
Child 2	So — the babies are born in the tropic sea? Then do they stay put? It makes sense to me.
Child 1	No. In March the bulls migrate north again. The cows stay behind with the calves and then
	Sometime in April the cows and their calves Migrate back to the Arctic on the same paths.
Child 2	Now I understand their reasons for migration. And their oceanic avenues of transportation.

Whales

Toothed or Baleen?

Whales are divided into groups by the way they catch their food. The two groups are the baleen whales and the toothed whales.

Baleen whales have special plates growing from their upper jaws. These plates are made of a material like your fingernails. The plates are in strips hanging down into the whale's mouth. The baleen strains food out of the water. Plankton is the food most often eaten by baleen whales. Plankton are very small plants and animals that live in the sea. A huge whale might eat several thousand pounds of plankton in a day.

Gray whale

Humpback whale

Toothed whales must chase and catch their food. They catch their food one piece at a time, usually eating fish, squid, or shellfish. Their sharp teeth are not used for chewing up food. The teeth grip the food while the whale tears its prey apart. Sometimes toothed whales swallow their food whole. The different toothed whales have teeth to fit their own needs. For example, the killer whale has large alternating teeth in its upper and lower jaws. When the killer whale closes its mouth, the teeth form a trap holding its prey securely.

Sperm whale

Killer whale

Bottlenose

Narwhal

List five baleen whales.

1._____

2._____

3._____

4._____

5._____

List five toothed whales.

1._____

2._____

3._____

4._____

5._____

List two ways a whale skeleton
is similar to your skeleton.

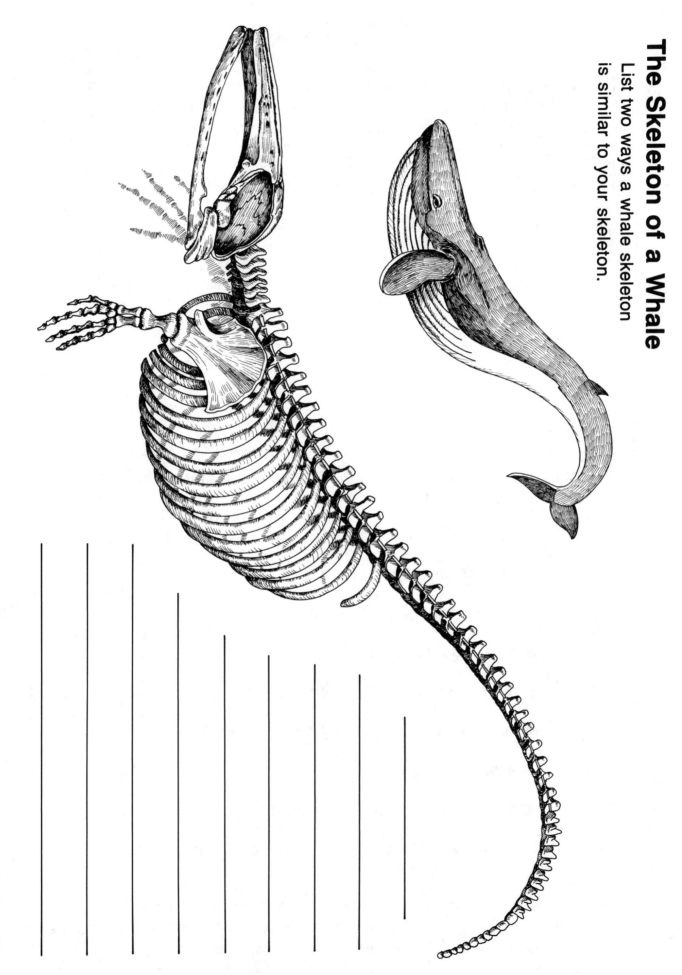

Back to the Sea

By studying ancient fossils and unborn baby whales, scientists think that whales have not always lived in the sea. Millions of years ago the ancestors of whales lived on land. They had four legs and were covered with fur. Over the years they moved further and further out into the ocean searching for food. Over millions of years their bodies changed into the sea mammals we see today.

What do you think the ancestors of whales looked like when they lived on land? Draw it here.

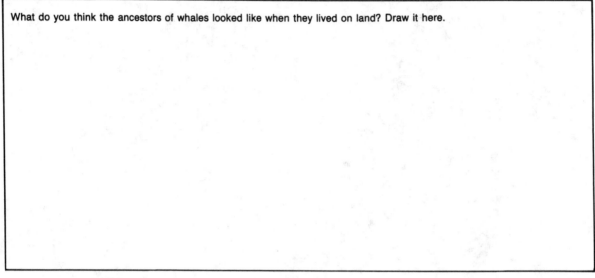

● body became streamlined

● hair disappeared

● blubber developed under the skin

● front legs became flippers

● back legs disappeared

● the tail widened to become flukes

● nostrils moved to the top of the head

● eyes became less important

● hearing became more important

● some lost their teeth and developed baleen

Find a partner. Discuss each of the changes in the list above. Decide why the change is helpful to a whale. For example, the body became stream-lined to make the whale a better swimmer.

Save the Whales

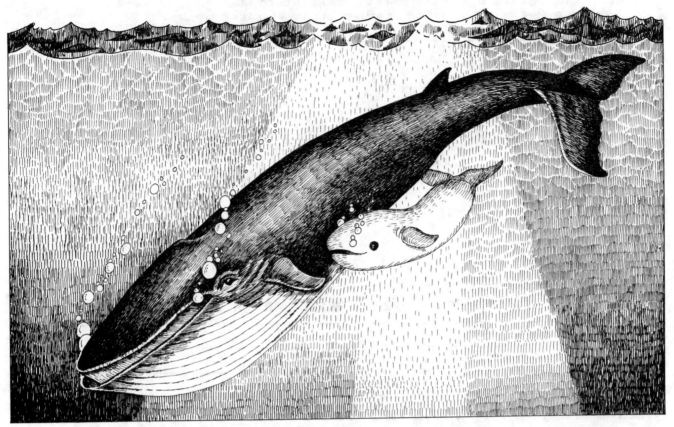

Although many whales are near extinction, there are still people who hunt them. Many groups of people are working to see that whale hunting ends. There have been laws passed to see that this happens.

Think about the questions listed below to help you decide how you feel about hunting endangered animals.

Do you think it is important to save an animal group from becoming extinct?

Do you think it is right to make laws saying which animals people can or cannot hunt?

Do you think it is all right for people to hunt these animals in order to feed their families?

Choose one of the following tasks to express your feelings about saving endangered animals.

- Make a poster.
- Write a speech.
- Design a bumper sticker.
- Write a letter to a friend.

Note: Reproduce this form to use with any whale as a simple reporting device. A child might do several pages (one for each type of whale studied) to create an individual book on whales. Have them draw their own illustrations or select a whale picture from the following two pages to paste onto their form.

A Whale Report

Name of whale

_____

_____

_____

_____

What does it look like? (color, size, special features)

_____

_____

_____

_____

Where does it live?

_____

_____

_____

_____

What does it eat?

_____

_____

_____

_____

Interesting facts about this whale:

_____

_____

_____

_____

Note: Reproduce these whales to use wherever you need a realistic illustration of a whale.

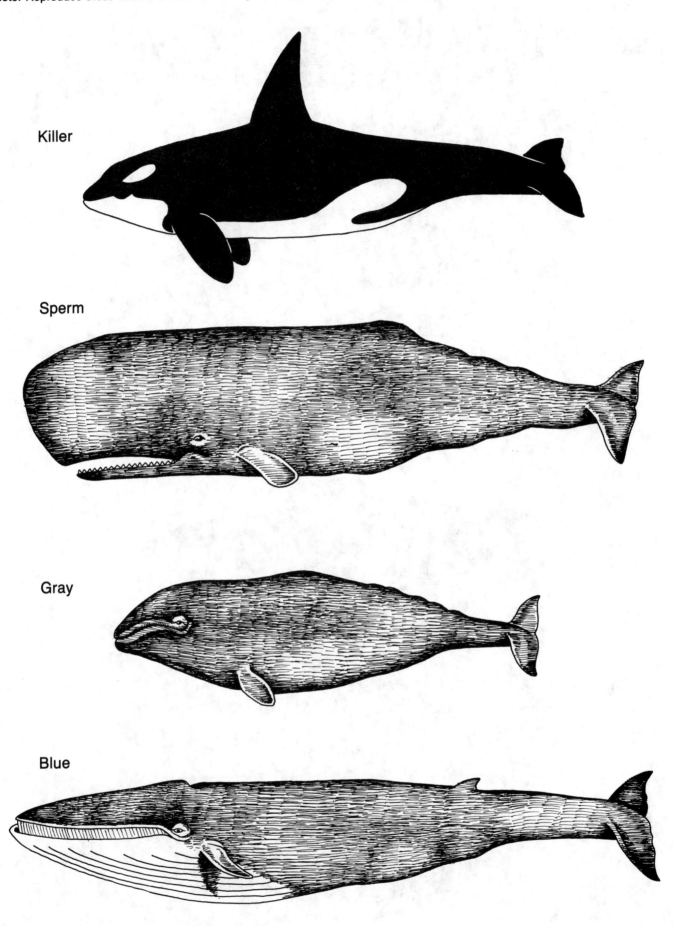

Killer

Sperm

Gray

Blue

Whales

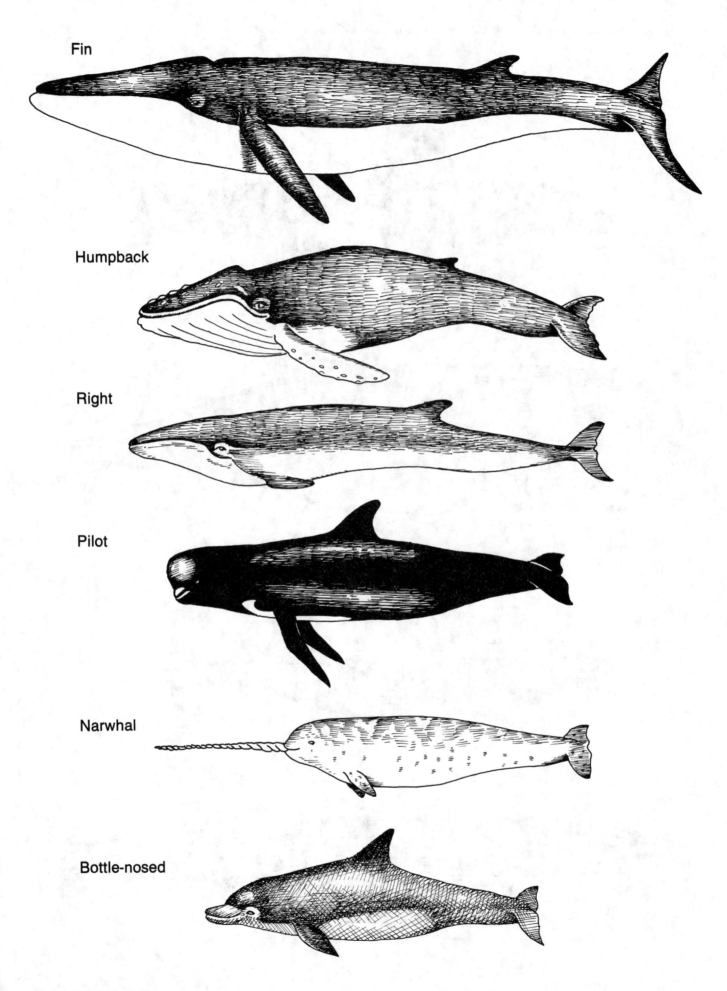

Fin

Humpback

Right

Pilot

Narwhal

Bottle-nosed

 Whales

Wondering About Whales

Discuss the question. Try to support your answer with facts.

 Should whales be captured and trained to perform in shows?

 Which do you think is more dangerous — a killer whale or a shark?

 Which do you think is smarter — a whale or a dog?

 Would you ever eat a whale roast?

 Is an enormous animal such as a whale better off on land or in the sea?

 Many types of whales are on the endangered list. Should Eskimos still be able to hunt them?

 Some countries have laws governing the killing of whales. Should there also be laws governing the killing of cows or pigs?

A Search for the Biggest and the Smallest

The Biggest

the biggest animal in the sea _____

the biggest animal on land _____

the biggest bird _____

the biggest planet _____

the biggest continent _____

the biggest _____

The Smallest

the smallest whale _____

the smallest mammal _____

the smallest bird _____

the smallest planet _____

the smallest continent _____

the smallest _____

Note: Have children work in groups of two to four to complete the listing activities below. Make available research tools such as dictionaries and atlases.

Think About It

Whales can be very large. Make a list of other words that mean very large.

1. _____

2. _____

3. _____

4. _____

5. _____

6. _____

7. _____

Whales are found in large bodies of water. List seas and oceans.

1. _____

2. _____

3. _____

4. _____

5. _____

6. _____

7. _____

A whale is a sea mammal. Make a list of other sea mammals.

1. _____

2. _____

3. _____

4. _____

5. _____

6. _____

7. _____

Whales move in interesting ways. Make a list of actions a whale might do.

1. _____

2. _____

3. _____

4. _____

5. _____

6. _____

7. _____

Turn this paper over if you need more room to complete your lists.

 Whales

Note: This activity is designed to help children create more interesting sentences.

Whales in Action

Brainstorm to create lists of words in the following categories.

Types of whales you might write about.

Words or phrases that describe how the whale looks:

    tell what the whale might do
    tell where the action takes place
    tell when the action takes place

Create oral sentences using words or phrases from each list.

> Example: The graceful humpback whale swam slowly through the still, dark sea singing its mysterious song all night long.

Have children write interesting sentences using words or phrases from each list. These sentences may be written on regular writing paper or on the form on the following page.

Reproduce a copy of the form for each child. They write their sentences on the lines, draw an illustration at the top, then cut the water line and fold up the bottom of the page. They will need to color in the water after folding the bottom of the paper up.

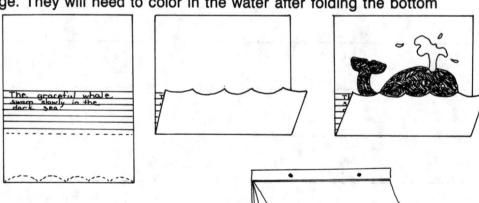

These pages may be put into a class book by stapling the pages into a cover.
Place the staples at the top of the page.

Whales

_____

_____

_____

_____

_____

Fold ——————————————————————————————————— Fold

cut

Conversations With a Whale

Each child will need a large sheet of drawing paper and a copy of the "speech bubbles" below.

Steps to follow:

1. Have your students think about this situation. "One afternoon you accidentally meet a talking whale. What would you ask the whale? What do you think his answer would be?"

2. Have children prepare their paper by cutting out the two speech bubbles. They must think about what they wish to draw and where the speech bubbles should go. Paste down the speech bubbles to the paper; then draw pictures of the whale and of themselves on the paper.

3. They write their questions and answers in the bubbles.

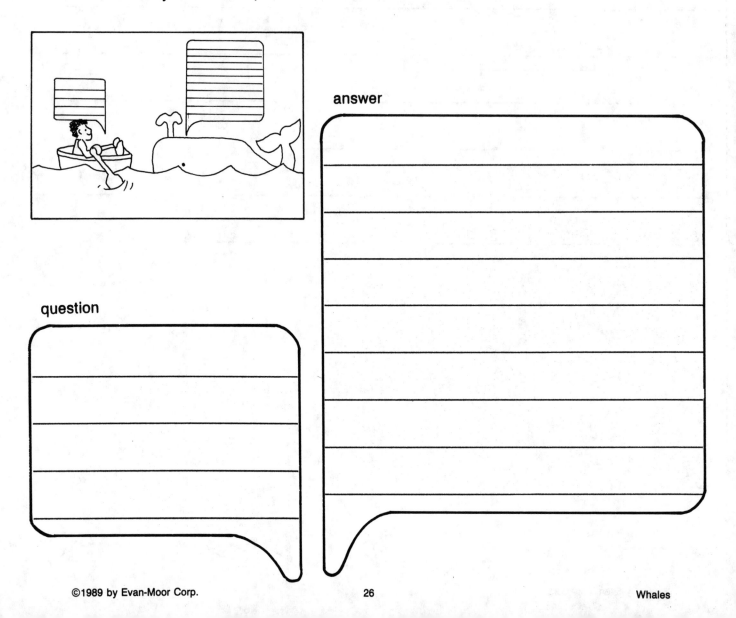

answer

question

Whales

A Whale of a Tail

Make a flap book following the directions on this page. Each student prepares one riddle (picture and words). Staple the finished pages together inside a cover.

Pages:

Give each student a 9" X 12" (22.9 X 30.5 cm) sheet of paper. Have them fold over one-third of the page to form a flap. They write their riddles on the left side of the paper and illustrate the answer under the flap, letting the animal's tail show.

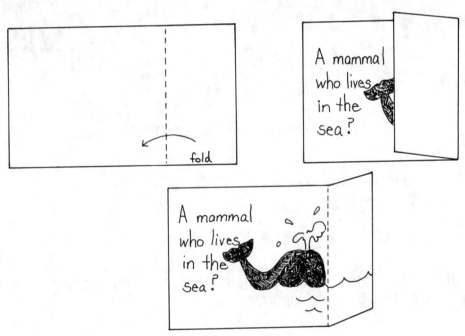

Cover:

Take two pieces of tag slightly larger than the children's papers. Make a hinge on the front cover and put the book together following these directions.

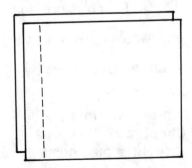

Cut a strip off the front cover.

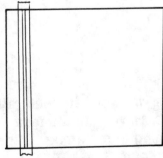

Tape the strip back to the cover piece. Leave a small space.

Staple the cover and the students' riddles together.

Note: Go through each of the steps listed below before requiring your students to write on their own. The more comfortable they are with the poetry form, the better the results will be. Second graders may not be ready to deal with counting syllables, but many can express a feeling within a short one-sentence format.

Whale Haiku

A haiku poem consists of seventeen unrhymed syllables organized into three lines.

> Line 1 — five syllables
>
> Line 2 — seven syllables
>
> Line 3 — five syllables

Most haiku poems refer to some element of nature. They express a moment of beauty which keeps you thinking or feeling.

In the beginning (for any grade level), it can be helpful to provide a simple guide that delineates the elements of the verse.

(Be sure your students understand that this is only one way of creating a haiku poem.)

where it happens..In the azure sea

what is happening..............................migrating whales swim slowly

when it occurs.....................................as the days pass by.

Do several examples together with your students. Brainstorm phrases that express each stage of the verse. Have your students select the phrases they wish to use. The most important thing to remember is that the thought should come first. Then adjust the syllable count.

When you feel your students are ready, have them create verses independently.

A Whale of a Poem

Sometimes it is fun to play with words in unusual ways to create a poem. Shape poems provide an opportunity for this type of experience.

Steps to follow:

1. Select a type of whale.

humpback

2. List descriptive words and phrases about the whale.

> enormous
> graceful
> musical
> swimming along
> singing a song
> dives into the sea
> jumps gracefully into the sky
> lifts its flukes in the sunlight
> dives deep into the dark sea

3. Select the ones you like best and arrange them so they have a pleasing sound.

the graceful humpback whale leaps gracefully into the sky, then dives deep into the dark sea singing a mysterious song

4. Draw the basic outline of the shape with black crayon or marking pen. Place a sheet of plain paper (ditto or typing) over the drawing. Fasten the pages together with a paper clip.

5. Write the words or phrases following the shape of the object to create the "shape" poem. Remove the top sheet of paper to see the completed poem.

What Does it Mean?
A Whale Crossword Puzzle

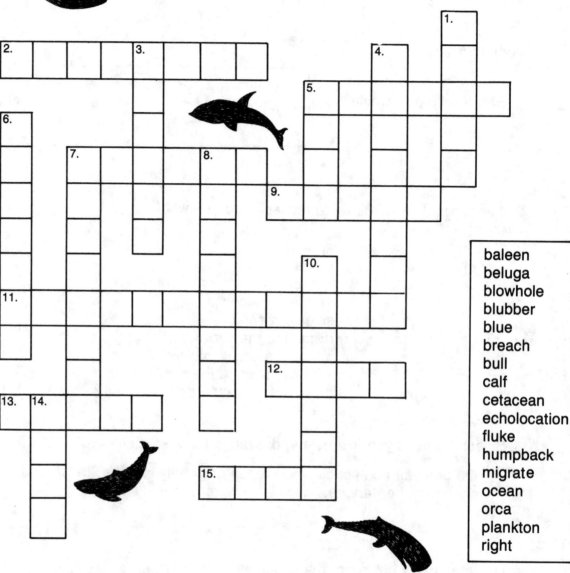

baleen
beluga
blowhole
blubber
blue
breach
bull
calf
cetacean
echolocation
fluke
humpback
migrate
ocean
orca
plankton
right

Across

2. this whale makes bubble nets
5. another name for the white whale
7. the word to use when a whale jumps out of the water
9. an end of a whale's tail
11. bouncing sound off an object to locate position
12. another name for the killer whale
13. the Pacific or Atlantic
15. the largest whale

Down

1. this whale's name is the opposite of left
3. some whales have this "sieve" instead of teeth
4. food for baleen whales
5. a male whale
6. the fat layer on a whale
7. a whale's nostrils
8. scientific name for all whales
10. seasonal travel from one location to another
14. a baby whale

Whales

A Sea Mammal Word Search

```
C O M M O N D O L P H I N F B W W D O
W A U P W H A L E Y B W K L R H H A T
H H L P Y G M Y A W O H I Y Y A A L R
U W A I W E B A T H W A L S D L L L I
M H E L F H E L P A H L L P E E E S S
P A W O E O A N U L E E E O S I F P S
B L H T E A R L E E A T R D W R I O O
A E A S P I N N E R D O L P H I N R S
C W L W A L L A I W H A L E A G W P D
K H E U L A W R W A W M W Z L H H O O
S W I M G A H W H T G H I H E T A I L
W H A L E A W H A L E R A N A P L S P
S P E R M W H A L E S E A L K L E E H
A L E B O T T L E N O S E Y E E E M I
Y A N G T Z E R I V E R D O L P H I N
```

BELUGA	MINKE
BLUE	NARWHAL
BOWHEAD	PILOT
BOTTLENOSE	PYGMY
BRYDE'S WHALE	RIGHT
CALIFORNIA GRAY	RISSO'S DOLPHIN
COMMON DOLPHIN	SEI
DALL'S PORPOISE	SPERM WHALE
FIN WHALE	SPINNER DOLPHIN
HUMPBACK	YANGTZE RIVER DOLPHIN
KILLER	

How many times can you find WHALE in this word search? _____

Draw a Whale

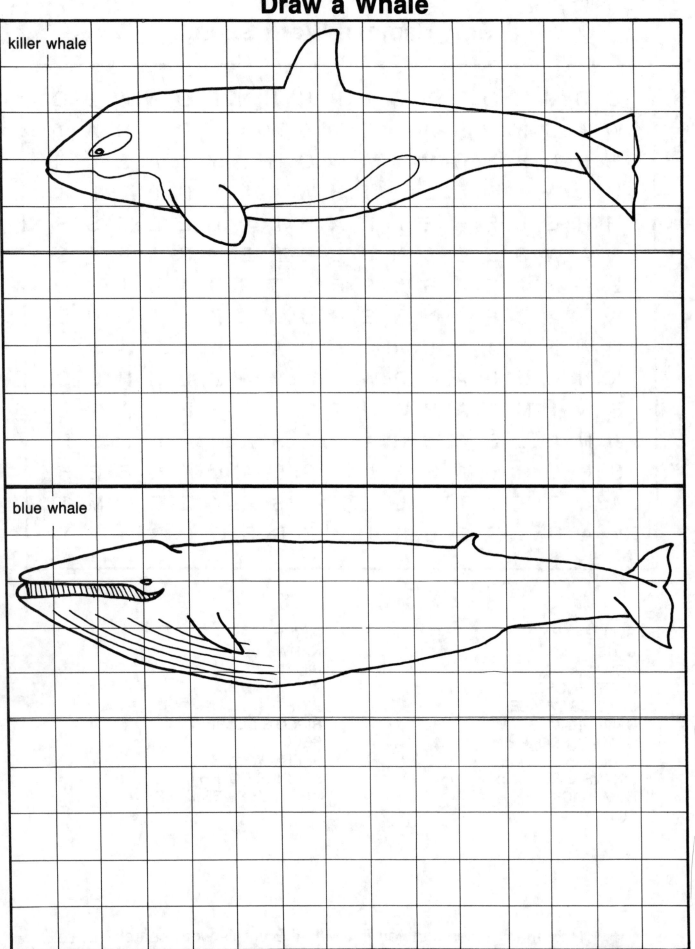

killer whale

blue whale

Whales

Paper Whales

Origami

Begin with a square piece of paper as large or small as you wish.
Follow these steps:

1.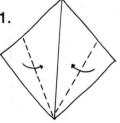

2.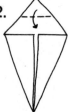

3.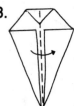

4.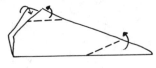

5.  Cut the tip of the tail a little bit.

6.  Finish off the face of the whale with pen or crayon.

Strip

Begin with a black or gray strip of construction paper 3'' X 18'' (7.6 X 45.7cm).
Follow these steps:

1.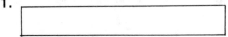

2.

3.  cut →

4.

5.

Draw eyes and mouth with black marking pen or crayon.

Add spouting water from a scrap of blue paper.

Fold and Cut

Begin with a 5'' X 18'' (12.7 X 45.7 cm) sheet of construction paper.
Follow these steps:

1. 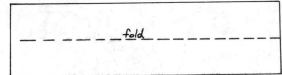 fold

3. Add a mouth and eyes with black marking pen or crayon.

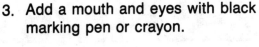

2.  cut   cut

Add spouting water from a scrap of blue paper.

Whale Bulletin Boards

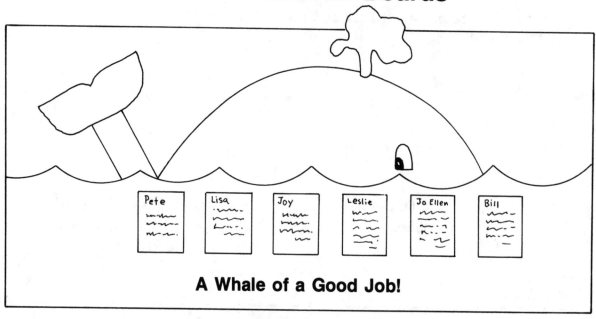

A Whale of a Good Job!

Cover your bulletin board with light blue butcher paper.
Cut simple basic shapes from gray or black butcher paper to create a large whale.
Add water cut from dark blue butcher paper.
The heading can be made from black paper or added to the background with black marking pen.

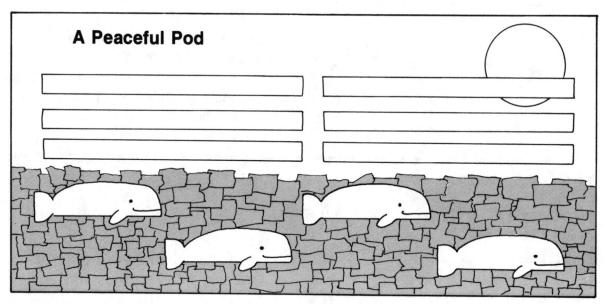

Cover your bulletin board with blue construction paper.
Add a yellow paper sun and a title cut from black paper.
Have your students cut black whales from butcher paper.
(The size will depend on the size of your bulletin board.)
Cover the lower half of the board (including the whales) with torn tissue paper in various shades of blue. Brush liquid starch over the tissue paper.
Put facts about whales on sentence strips. Add these to the upper half of the board.

Whales

Dot-to-Dot

Count by 2's

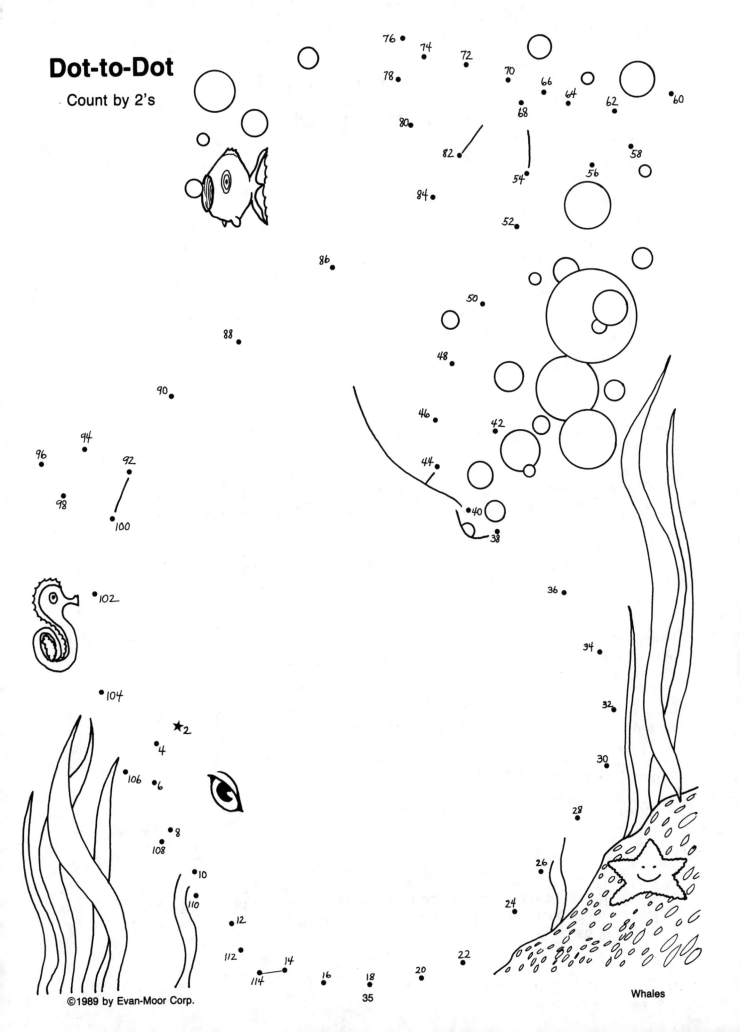

Whales

How Big is a Whale?
A Graphing Activity

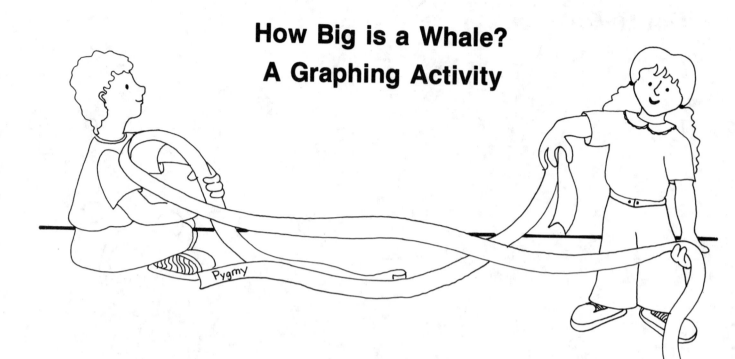

You will need a large area to do this activity (cafeteria, long hallway, playground, etc.).

Divide your students into groups. Assign each group a specific whale. Give them a roll of adding machine tape, a tape measure, and a black marking pen.

Each group is responsible for measuring out and labeling a strip of adding machine tape the length of their assigned whale. For example:

Humpback
62 feet (18.9 meters)

Humpback   62 feet

Gray Whale
50 feet (15.2 meters)

Gray Whale   50 feet

Pygmy Sperm Whale
11 feet (3.4 meters)

Pygmy 11 feet

Pin up the strips (or lay out on the playground) in the form of a bar graph. Have each group transfer the information to a graph form such as the one on the following page.

Whales

Note: Reproduce this form to use when graphing whale information such as length or weight. You may make changes before reproducing the form. Just cover the pictures and names of the whales with plain paper and add your own information.

A Whale Graph

fill in numbers						
name of graph						
	blue	narwhal	humpback	right	gray	sperm

Whales

Note: Take advantage of the interest in whales to practice word problems. Challenge your students to help you come up with good problems for their classmates to solve.

Whale Word Problems

Here are some sample word problems about whales. Select the ones appropriate for your students. Write one or two each day on the chalkboard. Have the students figure out the answers independently, then select someone to come to the board and explain how he/she determined the answer.

- A pilot whale is 28 feet long (8.5 meters). A narwhal is 20 feet long (6 meters). How much longer is the pilot whale?

- A blue whale calf drinks 130 gallons of milk a day. How much milk will it drink in two days?

- There are eight killer whales in the pod. The average weight of a killer whale is 16,000 pounds (7,258 kilograms). How much does the entire pod weigh?

- A common dolphin can swim 70 mph (113 km). How far could it swim in three hours?

- A newborn blue whale weighed two tons at birth. It gained ten pounds in an hour. How long did it take the baby to weigh three tons?

- A gray whale travels 6 mph (9.6 km). How long will it take the whale to travel the 5000 miles (8000 kilometers) from the Arctic to Mexico?

Open-Ended Activities to Use With Books About Whales

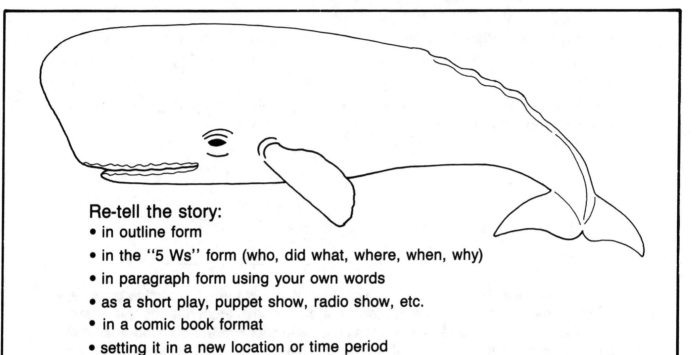

Re-tell the story:
- in outline form
- in the "5 Ws" form (who, did what, where, when, why)
- in paragraph form using your own words
- as a short play, puppet show, radio show, etc.
- in a comic book format
- setting it in a new location or time period

Share the book with others:
- give a book talk
- write a book review
- create an advertisement
- make a new book cover

Find examples of:
- cause and effect
- fact or fiction
- figures of speech
- descriptive language

Compare and contrast:
- characters within the story
- two books with a similar theme
- two books by the same author or illustrator

Describe:
- a character from the story
- a setting or location important to the story
- a feeling or mood
- one particular event

Amos and Boris
A Whale Book Project

Read Amos and Boris by William Steig to your class. (Older children may want to read the book for themselves.) Do one or more of the following activities with your students.

Origami Whales — Make the whale on page 33 extending the activity by adding water and Amos in his boat.

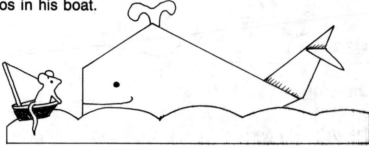

Dictionary Search — Use the rich vocabulary in this story to practice dictionary skills. Select ten or twelve words from the story. Have students find the words in the dictionary. After reading the definition, have them create sentences to show they understand the meaning of the word. This can be done orally or in written form. They might also look for the parts of speech, the diacritical markings, syllable divisions, etc.

enterprise
phosphorescent
luminous
immense
vast

Descriptive Language — Share samples of Steig's wonderfully descriptive language with your students before asking them to write on their own.

Compare and Contrast — Compare Amos and Boris to Aesop's The Lion and the Mouse.

 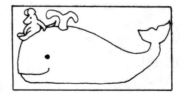

Rescue! — Amos called on his elephant friends to rescue Boris. Challenge your students to think of other ways to rescue a beached whale if you don't happen to have an elephant handy.

Note: The next three pages contain blank whale forms that can be used in many different ways across the curriculum.

Using Whale Activity Sheet Patterns

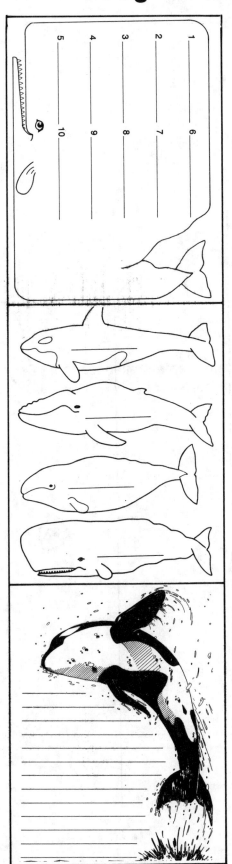

Page 42

- vocabulary lists of whale words
- spelling words appropriate to the whale unit
- words for a dictionary search activity
- homework assignments for a week
- language challenges

Page 43

- a math problem in each small whale
    computation
    counting challenges
    word problems
- riddles
- matching activities
- name tags or labels for folders/reports

Page 44

- write descriptive paragraphs or original poems
- handwriting practice
- cover art for a report or storybook
- list whale books read during the unit

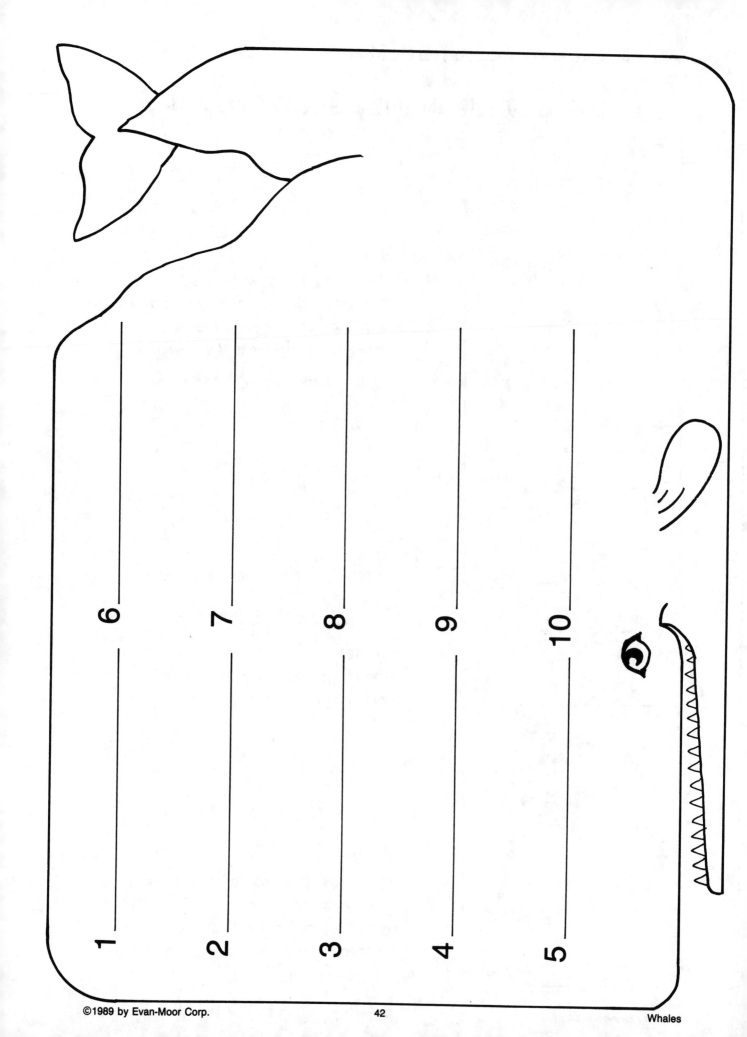

1

2

3

4

5

6

7

8

9

10

Whales

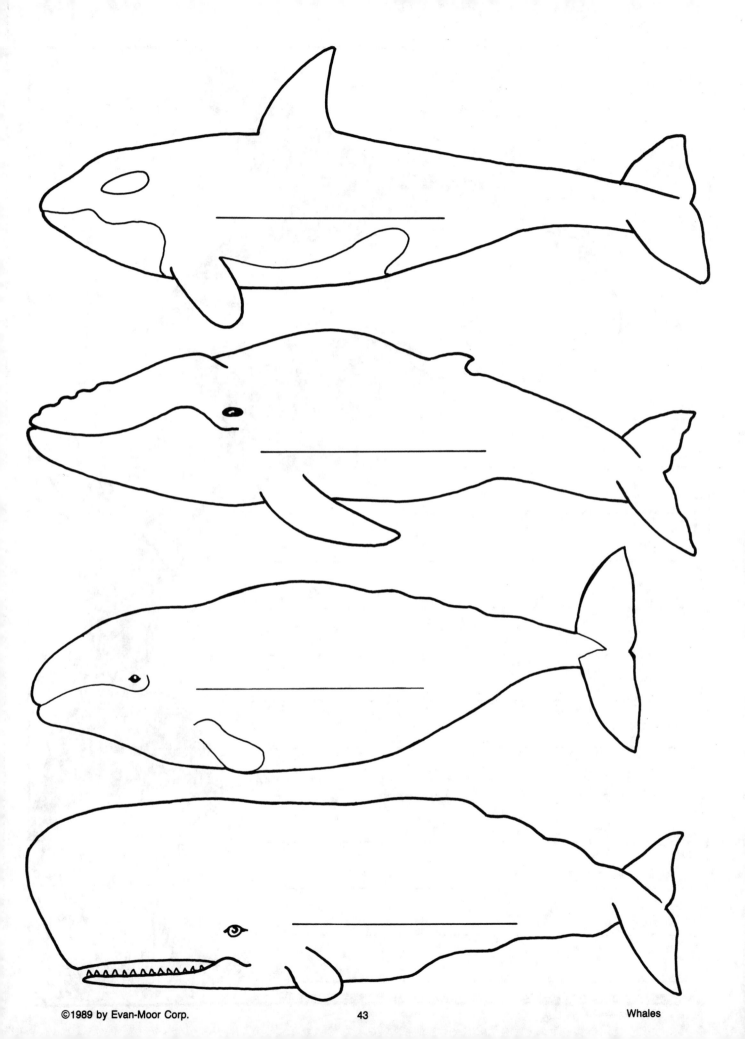

Whales

Did You Know?
A Skit About Whales
by Leslie Tryon

This science skit gives your children an opportunity to act out a comparison of whale sizes. The whales have been compared to the size of a school bus, something familiar to most school children.

All sizes are as close to the actual size as possible. School busses average between thirty and forty feet (9.2 X 12.2 meters) long.

Set: Arrange chairs in "school bus" rows. Children on the bus are the chorus. There are six individual whale parts. They are: the blue whale, the fin whale, the sperm whale, the gray whale, the killer whale, and the pygmy whale. Direct the individual whales to recite their lines, then "swim" on. All parts are in easy-to-learn couplet form.

Character	Dialogue
Chorus	The big yellow school bus, Full of curious kids like us,
	Drove right out to sea to see Just how big a whale can be.
	A giant of a whale swam right up to us and said...
The Blue	I'm the biggest whale. I'm the giant blue. The earth's biggest creature. It's absolutely true.
	From my fluke to my nose, a whale of a whale. The length of three busses, placed nose to tail.
Chorus	WOW! The big yellow school bus, Full of curious kids like us,

Continued on next page.

Script continued

Character	Dialogue
Chorus	Drove right out to sea to see Just how big a whale can be. Another big whale came speeding up to us and said...
The Fin	I'm the Fin. I'm fast 'cause I'm thin. Two and a half busses long from end to end. I have a bony moustache in place of teeth. Only in the top jaw, there's nothing underneath.
Chorus	Bigger than two school busses. WOW! The big yellow school bus, Full of curious kids like us, Drove right out to sea to see Just how big a whale can be. HEY! This one really LOOKS like a whale.
The Sperm	I'm the square-nosed Sperm whale. Two busses long, from my nose to my tail. I live in the tropics where there's lots to eat. But the giant squid is my favorite treat.
Chorus	Giant squid — Yuck!

Continued on next page.

Character	Dialogue

The big yellow school bus,
Full of curious kids like us,

Drove right out to sea to see
Just how big a whale can be.

LOOK! Here comes another one.

Gray Whale

I'm one school bus long. I'm the gray,
I'm bumpy all over, from barnacles they say,

I love to breach, to jump out of the sea
And you may see the whale lice, all over me.

Chorus

Whale lice — that's nice.

The big yellow school bus,
Full of curious kids like us,

Drove right out to sea to see
Just how big a whale can be.

Hey! Here comes a two-toned whale.

Killer Whale

I'm called the killer whale you know.
I'm dark on the top and light below.

I'm one of the very best hunters in the sea.
Your school bus is just a bit bigger than me.

Continued on next page.

Script continued

Character	Dialogue
Chorus	The big yellow school bus, Full of curious kids like us, Drove right out to sea to see, Just how big a whale can be. Can that little guy be a whale?
Pygmy Sperm	I'm only thirteen feet (about 4 meters) long, that's all. For a whale I guess I'm pretty small. I would fit in your bus. We could go for a ride. I could show you where the giant squid hide.
Chorus	Thanks very much, but we've got to get home. The big yellow school bus, Full of very smart kids like us, Met some whales and now we know, Just how big a whale can grow.

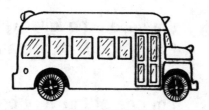

Whales